Foreword

There are those who may argue that Halifax is just another textile town nestling in a Pennine valley overlooked by all but those who live there.... But no! Not so. This is Halifax whose charms over the years have attracted some of the most significant names in commerce. At times, the home to the largest carpet manufacturer in the world as well as the largest building society. And, for many years, host to one of Britain's most respected ballet companies.

So why Halifax? The commercial acumen that caused Halifax to be recognised as a centre of commerce just goes from strength to strength. Yet the attractions of the late 20th century sit comfortably alongside their much older neighbours. EUREKA!, the award winning museum for children sits a mere stone's throw away from the Piece Hall, one of the architectural masterpieces of the 18th century and now a thriving outdoor marketplace attracting visitors from all over the world. Dean Clough, a phoenix from the ashes and a latter day success story known throughout the north of England, is the flourishing home for artists, artisans and the technology rising from the rubble of what used to be a decaying mill site. The list goes on..

For those who live and work in this remarkable town this book will bring to life that period of change which brought about the Halifax of today.

Read it and remember........

Alex Hall

Alex Hall - Presenter - The Alex Hall
Phone-In on the Pulse of West Yorkshire

First published in November 1995.
Revised and updated in October 1996 by:
TRUE NORTH PUBLISHING,
Dean Clough Industrial Park,
Halifax HX3 5AX. Tel (01422) 344344
Repro. by Transgraphic Ltd., Morley.
Printed by Joseph Ward Colourprint Ltd., Dewsbury.

true north
PUBLISHING

ISBN 1 900 463 05 9

£4.99 (Nett)

Contents:

Acknowledgements

There are many people who have influenced the compilation of this modest book, without whom, as the saying goes, it's publication would not have been possible. Stephen Gee, the well known author and collector of local photographs was good enough to edit the text and supply many of the photographs. Geoff Whippey supplied most of the modern scenes and Owen Sellers provided some excellent material from the Calder Valley - pictures taken by his late father J T Sellers. Thanks too to the advertisers - their support kept the price of this book to a reasonable level - and thanks also to Gareth Martin for organising the advertising content.

King Cross, taken about 1968; don't be misled by the old pick - up truck in the centre of the picture - it was part of a rally passing through the area - hence the interest shown by the family on the left of the photograph. These buildings were demolished as part of the new road scheme in the 1970s - they stood on the "Calder Valley" side of Wainhouse Road, opposite the road leading up to the moor. Looking at the width of the road here it is difficult to imagine it coping with the volume of traffic that the current by-pass does. *Picture: Geoff Whippey.*

The Old King at King Cross. This is *my* favourite picture in the whole book - though I never crossed its threshold. This local landmark was familiar to everyone making the journey down the Calder Valley from Halifax. In its way it was as much of an icon as Wainhouse Tower or the Piece Hall, with its familiar red neon sign glowing reliably at the junction. This picture was taken in the late 1960's - a clue to the date being the 1967 registration plate on the MGB parked across the car park entrance.   Sadly, the Old King was demolished in the seventies after over 100 years of trading. *Picture courtesy of Geoff Whippey.*

A tribute to Gladys

Several of the photographs in this book come from the "Gladys Lumb Collection" and I was delighted when Phil Holland of *True North Publishing* asked if I would write a tribute to Gladys. I first met Gladys some years ago when she literally walked into my back. I had put on an exhibition of old Halifax photographs at the Central Library and Gladys, using her magnifying glass (that many people will recall), was walking backwards whilst closely scrutinising the pictures. There followed, not surprisingly for those who knew Gladys, a lengthy conversation and a valued friendship. Gladys was a keen photographer and, as some of the pictures illustrate, a very able one. This, combined with her love of "talking" gave much pleasure to the countless clubs and organisations throughout the district that benefitted from her

Gladys and the long arm of the law at the Borough Market's Victorian promotion in December 1983.

Gladys pictured outside her father's shop in 1926

illustrated talks often assisted by her husband Harry. Gladys and Harry were married in 1940 and celebrated their golden wedding anniversary in 1990.

As a girl Gladys attended Clare Hall School. From there she went to work for her father, Tom Craven, in his shop at Regent House, Cross Hills, opposite the Grand Theatre. Spending her whole working life there, one could be forgiven for thinking she had led a somewhat sheltered life; no one who listened to her many stories would agree.

Apart from her photography Gladys had numerous interests. She was an excellent painter, loved dancing, whist drives, visiting museums, theatres, cinema's (particularly the REX for the organ recitals), the Maurice Jagger Centre, swimming (a sport

Gladys enjoyed into her 70s) and not least amongst many others, she loved travelling.

It was, perhaps, this latter "hobby" that made her life so interesting and "other" photographs reflect visits not only to every corner of Britain, but throughout the world. Her first trip on Concorde, taken at the age of 76, was followed by a return voyage on the QEII.

Gladys passed away earlier this year at the age of 87. She was a great "character" who will be sadly missed by everyone who knew her. Her photographs however, will continue to bring pleasure to all those who share the love she had for her home town, Halifax.

Stephen Gee.
September 1996

A 1916 photograph of Tom Craven's shop at North Bridge - with Gladys' mother Grace outside.

West Croft Mills, owned by Baldwin and Walker Ltd and sporting the sign "Ladyship Wools" pictured here in February 1974. This is another nostalgic scene captured by Gladys Lumb before the demolition mens hammers took it away forever in August 1977.

King Cross Street remembered........

These two views of what King Cross Street used to look like, before the demolition of most of these properties transformed the appearance of the area. The Burdock Way made a massive impact on the volume of traffic passing through the town centre when it was opened in 1973 after first being proposed as part of a plan to ease town centre congestion in 1947!
These photographs were taken by Gladys Lumb in 1968, a year before the bulldozers moved in. Thank goodness she had the foresight to record what most of us, at the time, would have considered to be scenes of very little interest. With the passage of thirty years or so they have acquired the power to rekindle many memories of life in our town.

Holt Brothers-Traditional Values in the Modern Age

In 1860 two brothers of the name Holt started a small business as Blacksmiths and Millwrights in Chatham Street amongst the packed streets of back-to-back houses of that time. They served the thriving textile mills and engineering companies in the town by making hand forgings, repairing textile equipment such as Beams and carrying out in the Blacksmith's Hearth the limited hardening that was required on such as cutting tools and chisels. Slowly, with the development of the Engineering industry and introduction of steels capable of being hardened to give improved wear resistance and strength, the Blacksmith's Hearth presented severe limitations to the service this small business, Holt Brothers, could offer to the local industries.

The beginning.......

.....the present day.

But 70 years after the establishment of this company it was the aim of the newly appointed manager that Holt Brothers (Halifax) Ltd should develop the service of the Heat Treatment of metals for the Engineering industry. Furnaces were installed for undertaking the wide range of heat treatment demanded for the phenomenal development taking place in engineering, and heat treatment became the sole service offered by Holts. Holt Brothers (Halifax) Ltd., having responded to the demands of engineers are now recognised as leading heat treatment metallurgists, offering the widest range of Heat Treatment and Coating services to the Engineering Manufacturing Industry throughout the UK.

Above: The whole of this book could be given over to the history of Dean Clough, the mill complex and family business which has played such a key role in the lives of thousands of Halifax families. Dean Clough dominated the industrial and economic landscape for over 100 years. John Crossley and sons Ltd. produced carpets at Dean Clough, employing up to 5000 people at the 40 acre site. The mill operated virtually as a small town in its own right, with independent generators for electric power, an army of craftsmen and engineers from every trade imaginable, and substantial railway sidings from which Crossley's quality carpets were despatched to every corner of the globe.

Above right: The nineteen men captured here in this picture from about 1912 were workers at the Halifax abattoir. The boy in the foreground looks too smartly dressed for what must have been a very messy job. The parcels under his arm suggest an errand in process; few people would have missed the opportunity to be included in a photograph when the chance occurred.

Right: The picture here shows the inside of the machine shop at Wright Electric Motors Ltd in 1929. At this time the company was situated on Pellon Lane, at the site now occupied by a retail park.

Above: First Avenue, Manor Drive. An autumn day in 1908 and three boys pose for this photograph. The boy in the middle may have been employed as a grocer's boy, judging by his long white apron. Typical of the time is the fact that each boy is wearing a cap, notably not the baseball variety of today's youth.

Below: Hipperholme is seen here in this scene from 1949. The shop on the right is J. Riley, grocer, herbalist and booking agent for Hebble Buses. The van in the foreground is delivering Jacob's Cream Crackers and the mother and daughter passing the bottom of Whitehall Street are no doubt on their way to buy groceries from the same parade of shops.

Above right: Skircoat Green at the turn of the century saw these four little girls photographed playing on St. Anne's Road. These substantial terraced houses have changed little since those times but the road surface had improved beyond recognition. At around the time when this picture was taken changes were being made in the way that education was organised. In 1902 local education authorities were enabled, by an act of Parliament, to organise secondary school education and became accountable to the town council. In 1903 the School Board passed control of the town's 24 schools and 13,500 pupils over to the new authority. Skircoat Township, which included Skircoat Green, Pye Nest and Copley, was incorporated into the Borough of Halifax in 1899.

Above: August 1934 was the postmark on this postcard sent from King Cross. Tramlines are still clearly visible, as are the ornate tram standards carrying the electric power for the vehicles. A single decker coach can be seen making its way out of King Cross towards Sowerby Bridge or the Calder Valley. Within five years the motor bus was to take the place of trams which had served the town since 1898. The public house in the background is the Old King, knocked down in the 1970's after over 100 years of business to make way for the new road scheme.

Above left: Ovenden Road in the 1930's. A sea of granite cobble stones took local traffic to and from the town centre, and a busy tramway carried passengers up and down the cobbled slopes for almost 40 years.

Left: This aerial photograph shows King Cross in 1930. Wainhouse Tower can be seen on the left of the picture rising some 250 feet above the hillside overlooking Sowerby Bridge. The Tower was constructed in 1870 by J.E. Wainhouse at a cost of ten thousand pounds. Its purpose was to act as a chimney for smoke from Wainhouse's Dyeworks some 250 yards down the hillside.

Below: The Packhorse Bridge, in Hebden Bridge, is the setting for this delightful picture - *courtesy of The Prospect Inn, Halifax.*

Right: Victoria Buildings, Luddenden Foot decorated for the Jubilee celebrations in 1935. The buildings were the home of Martins Bank for many years and began life as the Victoria Hotel. *Photo courtesy J.T. Sellers.*

Left: The sharpness of this photograph from 1910 belies the fact that is over 80 years old. Tram lines can clearly be seen on the cobbled road along with the buildings at the end of Higgin Lane which later became the post office. *Photo courtesy Prospect Inn.*

Below: High Street, Luddenden about 1930. Luddenden post office complete with telegraph service is advertising Wall's Ice and "Fresh Palethorpe's Sausages". The small wheeled pram may look strange when compared with today's equipment but it was typical of the era. *Photo by J.T. Sellers*

Below: The paddling pool at Luddenden Foot is pictured here in this 1930's photograph. W. Horsfall and sons, the local cart, van and wagon builders, can be seen on the left of the picture and Luddenden Foot Congregational Church clock tower can just be made out in the background. *Picture by J.T. Sellers.*

Right: Towngate, Southowram at the turn of the century. Southowram's post office can be seen advertising Stephen's Ink and the sign on the left of the window says "John Crossley, Newsagent and Stationer". The window immediately on the right of the post office was a grocers of the same name. *Picture courtesy of The Prospect Inn.*

Bottom right: Halifax Lane, Luddenden from Carrfield in the mid 1920's. The two large buildings on the left of the picture are the Beauvoir Works and nestling below them the joinery and undertakers business of H. Hall can be seen. *Picture by J.T. Sellers.*

Left: Ripponden Village was a considerably quieter place in 1913 than it is today, judging by this photograph of the time.

Below left: A quiet day in Sowerby Town is captured beautifully in this photograph from 1938. The only vehicle in view (other than the bicycle which can just be made out in the centre right of the picture) is the bread delivery van shown with its doors open. Using a magnifying glass may reveal individual loaves of bread about to be delivered to the houses and farms roundabout. The peaceful scene would be shattered only a year later by the start of the Second World War.

Below: Tramcar at Belmont, Sowerby Bridge: This tramcar, number 60, is shown here en-route to Triangle near Belmont Terrace in Sowerby Bridge. The tramway from Halifax to Sowerby Bridge came into service late in 1902 and was extended to serve Triangle some three years later. This photograph dates from around 1910.

Left: This 1920's solid-tyred flat backed lorry was owned by H. Hellewell and Co. of Holme Royd Mills in Luddenden Foot. It is seen decorated here for the Halifax Infirmary Gala. Hellewells were worsted spinners in Luddenden Foot until 1972.
Picture: J.T. Sellers.

Below: This very early tramcar built in 1898 was one of the first to be brought into service in Halifax. It operated on the route between Cow Green and Pellon. Halifax was one of the first northern industrial towns to begin an electric tramway system. The last tram route, to Ovenden, ceased in February 1939.

Left: Single decker buses making the journey up and down the hill to Midgley have been a feature familiar to many people for over 60 years. The first bus service from Midgley is seen here passing Solomon Hill in 1928.

Right: This very smart Bedford seven tonner - KWU768 dates from 1951 and was operated by Ripponden & District Motors (now known as Ripponden Carriers). At that time the company used to advertise its other business activity - buses and coaches - and an advertisement is seen here for the world's first half deck coaches - seen below on this page.

Below right: This Leyland Titan double decker was new in 1930 and was one of several operated by John Hirst Snr. who started the company in 1921. At the time this photograph was taken the company was moving into the parcel business. Parcels eventually became the main core business, and the firm sold the buses to the Corporation before the Second World War. Coaching remained part of the firm's activities until the late '50s.

Below: A 1952 AEC Mark IV in metallic blue and grey with a very rare half deck body, pictured here when it was delivered to the company.

Photographs on this page courtesy of Ripponden Carriers.

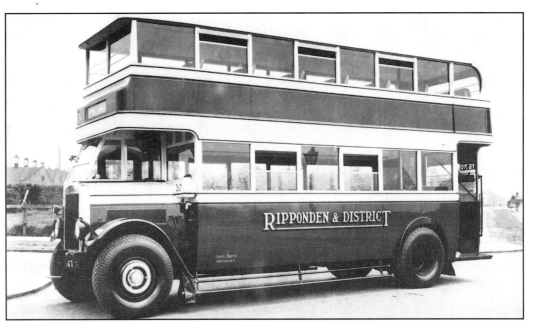

Left: This Shire Horse and Dray pictured here at the end of Harrison Road would have been a familiar sight in Halifax as it delivered barrels of beer for T. Ramsden and Son Ltd. of the Stone Trough Brewery.

Below left: This picture shows three carriages awaiting passengers at Sowerby Bridge Railway Station in 1872. A rail service had been in place for over thirty years by the time this photograph was taken. The railway age caused the rapid decline of Canal Transport in the town.

Below right: A Corporation single decker at the bottom of King Edward Street.

Above: The opening of the first tramcar service to Brighouse in February 1904 resulted in this picture. The first local tram services began in June 1898. By the time that this picture was taken, the services to King Cross, Highroad Well and Hebden Bridge were already established.

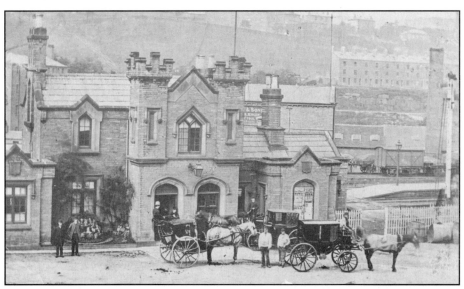

Below: Frank Ford is a well known name to everyone who has ever bought fish and chips. Fish frying ranges have been produced at their Sovereign works for many decades. This picture, dating from the 1930s, was supplied by Frank Ford.

Right: A Leyland Bison from 1932 - soon after the parcel side of the business was started by John Hirst Snr. of Ripponden and District Motors.

Bottom Right: These two waggons - number 13 and 14 are parked up for the camera outside T.E Short's removal business on Union Street South.

Right: Long before the advent of smokeless zones and pollution control, the effect of many decades of soot deposits can be seen on the Town Hall. The building itself dates from 1863 and was designed by Sir Charles Barry. The building on the right of the picture was constructed for Burton's the tailors in 1932, and its top floor was once the location of the Empress Ballroom.

Below: A good impression of what the local atmosphere would have been like in 1950's Halifax is given by this photograph. There are around 50 mill chimneys in the picture, not to mention the emissions from the railway, gasworks and domestic dwellings. Little wonder that the buildings appear so uncharacteristically black to the modern eye.

Left: Halifax in wartime is caught on camera in this view from 1943. The distinctive livery of the two double decker Halifax Corporation Buses make the scene unmistakably local, and steam can be seen rising from "Salt" and "Pepper", the town's two cooling towers, if further proof were needed. "Bull Green" is thought to be derived from the practice of bating bulls with dogs during the sixteenth century. The area later served as a cattle market- giving rise to another theory about the origin of its name.

Below left: The area known as Old Market was once used by local traders operating from stalls set up in the busy street. The activity was mirrored in Market Street and Corn Market from the earliest recorded years of commerce in the town until an act of Parliament in 1810. The basic fabric of the area has changed little since this picture was taken. Freeman Hardy & Willis, the famous shoe retailer no longer occupies this fine building, but the Union Cross public house (the longest established in the town) is still going strong. Millets, Burton, Shaw Hardcastle and Mitchell's Outfitters will be fondly remembered by many Halifax people.

Below: The Cross Field bus station and Odeon cinema about 1960.

Left: This atmospheric scene shows Commercial Street and the Post Office in 1912. The fine Victorian and Edwardian architecture that characterises the area has changed little over the years. Development began here towards the end of the century, with the Post Office itself being based on this spot from 1887 before being enlarged in 1926 to make room for the telephone exchange. The building towards the right of the picture later housed the headquarters of the Halifax Building Society and was built in 1904.

Below: This view of Southgate dates from 1897. It depicts an era when horse - drawn vehicles ruled the roads and gas lamps lit the main streets around the town. A year before this picture was taken the Borough Market had been opened by the Duke and Duchess of York. The clock tower of the Town Hall can just be made out in the background - it had been built 24 years earlier in 1873.

Below left: The Victoria Hall - in the centre of this picture - opened in 1901 and was run as a commercial undertaking until 1960 when it was taken under the wing of the Corporation. The Picture House, on the left, was one of the venue's main competitors. The Victoria Hall has survived as a local entertainment landmark for almost 100 years despite the many cultural and technological changes that have affected Halifax.

Right: New Year's Day in 1779 saw the opening of one of Halifax's best known landmarks. The Piece Hall originally functioned as a market place for handloom weavers to sell their "pieces" of cloth. The sheer scale of the building is testament to the massive importance of the cloth manufacturing trade to the area. 315 individual rooms and the enormous open courtyard were the focal point of local cloth trading. The advent of mills, made possible by water and steam power, caused a sharp decline in home manufactured cloth. Consequently, the Piece Hall's importance as a centre for textile trade was quickly eroded. In 1868, less than 100 years after it was opened, it was taken over by the Halifax Corporation and used as a wholesale market for fruit, vegetables and fish. The Piece Hall's special place in the affections of the townspeople of Halifax was secured in the 1970's when it was restored and revitalised by the local authority. It now acts as a focal point for many retail and recreational activities and is visited and enjoyed by people from all over the world.

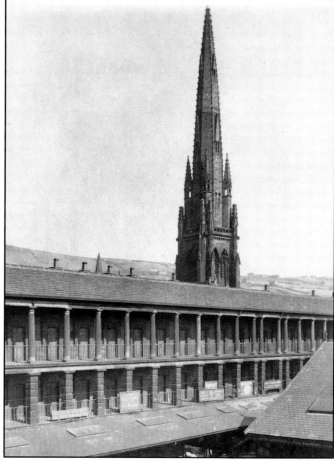

Left: King Edward Street looking up to Commercial Street. This picture was taken in the 1930s. Taylors the chemists occupied the large corner property which is now the location of the Co-op. The bus stop for the Sowerby service is located outside F.W. Woolworths and the sign for the Alexandra Restaurant can just be made out a little further up the street.

This photograph taken around 1967, captured the sprawling railway goods yard in the heart of industrial Halifax before it was swept away just a few years later. The coal yard was still in use when this picture was taken, but the drive towards a cleaner environment soon made them virtually redundant. Along with the general clearance that took place across this flat piece of land in the valley bottom two other landmarks - the cooling towers nicknamed "salt and pepper" were soon to be demolished to further change the landscape here. Today, much of the land shown behind North Bridge is taken up by the Leisure Centre and its surrounding car parking area. The present two span iron bridge that is North Bridge was opened in 1872, replacing the former stone bridge which had served the area for 100 years. *(Photo courtesy of Geoff Whippey)*

Another view of Halifax from 1967. Most of the property in the foreground was pulled down to accommodate the Burdock Way. Much of the visible area belonging to Dean Clough Mills has been cleared now - and the chimney in the foreground demolished. The Cock o' the North brewery went the same way and the area has now taken on a much cleaner, though less characterful, appearance. Far away in the background of the picture a crane can just be made out at the construction site which became the flats at Shaw Hill near the Shay football ground. *(Picture Geoff Whippey)*

This photograph from 1968 is guaranteed to bring back memories of shopping in Halifax before the days of the Woolshops development. The New Talbot and the Sun Inn have long gone - along with the Abattoir (the building half way down the picture on the left) and the sea of cobble stones which characterised this part of town. *Picture courtesy of Geoff Whippey.*

This picture captures the atmosphere of Dean Clough at the time, in the late 1960s, when it was slipping from maturity into decline. Few people could have predicted then that the buildings shown here would be rejuvenated and revitalised within 20 years to become the home of scores of new enterprises in the town. A fitting role for this marvellous local landmark.
Picture: Geoff Whippey.

Bull Green gardens, circa 1959; there have been many subtle but significant changes to the area since this picture was taken.

Below: Thirty women - regulars at the Prospect Inn - the public house which enjoys a panoramic view of the heart of Halifax from Range Bank - are captured for posterity on this photograph. The story behind the picture is unknown - but the clues are all there. Was it the end of a happy day out in Blackpool? - the hats worn by seven of the ladies suggest something of the sort.

Below, right: Fairgrounds were a popular and much looked - forward - to diversion in the 1930s. This ride - The Super Noahs' Ark - was part of William Shaw's travelling fairground company, seen here in Elland in 1932.

Above: Crow Wood Park bowling green has always been a well used facility in the Pye Nest area of Sowerby Bridge. It is seen here in 1939. Crow Wood Park was initially opened in 1923 - partly to act as a memorial to the First World War.

Above: This scene was captured in Ripponden in 1931. Day excursions to the coast were a popular pastime sixty years ago with the people of Calderdale; this was the era of the motor coach - trams were rapidly being superseded by this form of transport, and increasingly reliable vehicles and better roads meant that longer journeys could be undertaken with confidence. The buses featured here are Leyland Tigers - popular with operators for many years. These pictured in Ripponden were used by Ripponden and District Motors on the routes displayed on the side of the coaches - Manchester - Oldham - Denshaw - Sowerby Bridge and Halifax. Interestingly, the boy pictured second from the left is John Hirst Junior - "young John" as he was known when he became managing director of the company some forty years later.
Picture kindly supplied by Ripponden Carriers.

Above: This charming scene depicts four twelve year old boys next to the Maypole in Warley. They are reading an article about Wilfred Pickles of "Have A Go" fame - a former resident of Warley who was about to transmit the programme from his native village. Edward Riley, the boy seen second from the left here, was showing a particular interest in the Courier. This proved prophetic - he later became the paper's editor! *Picture kindly supplied by Margaret Holland.*

Right: The reservoir at Ogden has always been a local beauty spot popular with Halifax townspeople since it was constructed in 1858. When it was first added to the water resources of the town it enabled many areas to receive a reliable water supply for the first time. At the time of its' construction over 100 years ago the reservoir held 200 *million* gallons of water and cost the ratepayers nearly £100,000.

Below: Halifax Zoo. Young people today can be hard to impress, but most will, however, raise an eyebrow on hearing that Halifax once had its very own zoo - with real life elephants and lions - as long ago as 1909.

The Halifax zoo and amusement park was situated at Chevinedge, Exley - and opened just three months before this picture was taken. The list of facilities at the zoo was impressive; countless exotic animals, as well as a theatre, miniature railway and extensive catering facilities. A bear escaped from the zoo in 1913 and caused havoc in the area for two hours before being recaptured by a keeper. Sadly, the zoo proved to be too far ahead of its time and was forced into closure just five years after it opened.

Below: Sunny Vale was a popular, commercially operated amusement park. It is seen here at the turn of the century being enjoyed by hundreds of local people. The pleasure park in Hipperholme covered over 40 acres and drew up to 100,000 visitors every year between 1843 and the late 1940s.

Sunny Bunces' - as it was known to most Halifax (and district) people was the nineteenth century equivalent of today's Alton Towers. Access to the park was typically by rail as the grounds were within easy walking distance of Hipperholme railway station.

Above: Shibden Park has played a part in the lives of thousands of Halifax people over the years. Shibden - a name derived from the words *sheep dene* - opened as a park relatively recently in terms of the history of Halifax. The Prince of Wales planted a tree there to mark the occasion in 1926. Shibden Park was a gift to the citizens of Halifax from Mr A S McCrea - the son of a former Mayor of the town.

Most of the parks in Halifax were opened as a consequence of land being donated by wealthy local figures. Shibden was one of the last parks to opened, the dates for the other major parks are: People's Park, 1857; Savile Park, 1866; Shroggs Park, 1881; Akroyd Park, 1887 and West View Park 1905.

Manor Heath was purchased by the Halifax Corporation in 1929 for the sum of eighteen and a half thousand pounds.

97.5 & 102.5 FM

PROUD TO BE YOUR LOCAL STATIONS IN WEST YORKSHIRE

Local news, travel and weather service plus good music across West Yorkshire

COMPETITIONS - LOCAL SPORT - OUT AND ABOUT IN YOUR LOCAL COMMUNITY

Hear the Alex Hall Phone - in on The Pulse

Northgate was a very different place when this photograph was taken by Gladys Lumb in 1975. Most of us will remember trips to *Willis's* and their slogan "bargains are our business". This block was demolished in 1979 to make way for the new council buildings, Northgate House, and our marvellous Central Library.

Round and about Old Halifax

Attractively framed sepia tone prints reproduced from the "Gee" collection. Over 12000 photographs from all over Calderdale. To view and order please telephone 01422 370641 or 01422 823999